EY AROUND THE WORLD?

CREATE

GET CREATIVE!

A jet fighter, a cute pug or an ice dragon – you can build anything you like with your LEGO® bricks. On special trading cards you'll find exciting building challenges that put your skills to the test. Are you a master builder? Grab your LEGO® bricks and let's find out! Use your imagination to build even more amazing creations than the ones on the cards!

003

WHEELBARROW
A wheelbarrow comes in quite handy if you want to transport potatoes, for example. Can you build a pot to cook these spuds?

115

ICE DRAGON
Puffy the little ice dragon has lost all his dragon eggs. Built him some nice eggs in different colours. That should help this hot head keep his cool!

012

SCARECROW
So far today, the Scarecrow has scared seventeen crows away from the corn field! Time to turn the tables – build something terrifying to scare the Scarecrow!

JET FIGHTER
This futuristic jet fighter is a seriously speedy machine! Build an obstacle course with your bricks, then navigate through it as fast as possible!

009

TRACTOR
Every farmer needs a tractor to help haul all those tasty cereals to the mill. Grab your bricks and build a little windmill!

COLLECT THEM ALL!

LEGO® Create The World TRADING CARDS are available exclusively from Sainsbury's. Shop in store or online between 6th May and 16th June 2020 to start collecting.*

An easy way to store them all!
This collector's album will allow you to store and secure your cards as well as to play with them anytime you like!

Follow these simple instructions!
Every card space has two slots. Insert the matching card in the top left and bottom right slots. This way you can fix cards on both sides of each page and access them quickly.

Got every card?
Check which ones you're missing on pages 58-59!

FACTS!

ON THIS MINDBOGGLINGLY AMAZING TRIP YOU WON'T JUST HAVE GREAT FUN; YOU'LL ALSO LEARN A THING OR TWO ABOUT FAR AWAY PEOPLE, EXTRAORDINARY ANIMALS AND LAST BUT NOT LEAST A GREAT DEAL ABOUT YOURSELF AND YOUR BODY – HOW IT WORKS, WHAT IT NEEDS AND HOW TO STAY HEALTHY! LET'S GO!

*Subject to availability and exclusions apply. Available in Sainsbury's supermarkets, centrals, locals and Sainsburys.co.uk. Online shops delivered by 16th June.

START YOUR ADVENTURE NOW!

DISCOVER THE WORLD WITH ALL ITS INTERESTING AND DELICIOUS FACTS!

From Europe's potatoes and grains, via Asia's tasty spices to America's hot chilli peppers: The world is a vast place and vast is the range of ingredients on each continent. Come with us on a marvellous tour and learn about all the things the planet has to offer. Oh, and while you're at it, you can solve all the brain teasers!

ADVENTURE ➤

Did you know?

Brain teaser

LET'S GO ON A RIDE, LILY!

I'M RIGHT WITH YOU, SAM!

CONTENTS

ALL ABOARD, PLEASE!

SAM

Hobbies: Mental exercise, cooking with Lily, eating his favourite dishes, playing memory games
Favourite ingredients: Cream cheese, potatoes, chilli peppers
Favourite cuisine: Thai & Italian
Role model: Stephen Hawking & all hard working chefs

1

Brain teaser

IMAGINE YOURSELF MAKING TOAST. FIRST YOU PUT A SLICE OF BREAD INTO THE TOASTER. WHILE IT'S TOASTING, YOU GET THE JAM OUT OF THE REFRIGERATOR AND A PLATE FROM THE CABINET. WHEN THE TOAST IS READY, YOU PUT IT ON THE PLATE. YOU PUT JAM ON THE TOAST AND SPREAD IT. FINALLY, YOU'RE READY TO EAT. **WHAT WAS THE FIRST THING YOU DID JUST NOW?***

LILY

Hobbies: Sports, reading, travelling, playing Mau-Mau
Favourite ingredients: Carrots, butter, tofu
Favourite cuisine: English & Indian
Role model: Prehistoric humans who invented cooking

LET'S START ON A FARM WITH TATTIES, SAM!

IF I CAN GET SOME OF THEM ON A PLATE!

2

SPUDS FOR YO[U]

CREATE

3

There are more than 1,000 different varieties of potato worldwide

PRECIOUS POTATOES

The unassuming spud has changed Europe more than any monarch could ever dream of! When the Spaniards brought them back from America more than 400 years ago, potatoes were soon adopted to some people's diet. The potato averted famines and helped populations survive and grow because they provided energy. Before long, all of Europe was chowing down on this little root vegetable.

WHOA, DUDE! THOSE SPUDS SOUND AWESOME!

4

Potatoes are sometimes harvested using multiple tractors

HARVEST BEGINS IN SUMMER

Growing potatoes is an exciting business. No, really! Potatoes are a very easy-going kind of vegetable. They'll grow happily in just about any well-drained soil. Then, come August, the UK is criss-crossed by both huge combine harvesters and humble wheelbarrows, all working tirelessly to unearth the nation's favourite root veggie. Over 31 kilograms of potatoes are munched by every Brit annually – that's 600 grams a week!

R TUMMY!

WHEN THE SPANIARDS BROUGHT THIS HUMBLE VEGETABLE BACK WITH THEM FROM SOUTH AMERICA, IT STILL TOOK SOME TIME UNTIL IT SPREAD TO COOKING POTS ACROSS EUROPE: FARMERS ARE HAPPY TO THIS DAY ABOUT THOSE SPUDS!

7

> I KNEW I SHOULDN'T HAVE EATEN THOSE LEAVES!

BOIL IT, STEAM IT, FRY IT!

After gaining access to potatoes, people first had to figure out how to prepare them. When spuds first arrived in Europe, we tried to eat them raw. And while that's not exactly dangerous, it certainly makes for a bitter and indigestible meal! After a while, folks realised it was better to boil, steam or fry them. Given heat and a little patience, the potato is a super tasty food and a good source of B vitamins, fibre and energy. However, it's worth noting that its leaves, flowers, sprouts and fruits are poisonous.

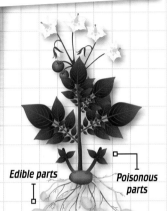

Edible parts

Poisonous parts

How about designing your own coat of arms?

> TIME TO SWAP MY BRUSH FOR A POTATO, MAYBE? HMMM?!

EAT ME, PRINT ME!

Ever heard of potato printing? Our resident artist assures us that it's jolly good fun! All you need are some spuds in different shapes and sizes. Cut them in half and draw your favourite design into the freshly-cut edge (the first letter of your name perhaps?). Then ask your parents to cut around the outline with a knife. Let the potato dry, apply a coat of paint and put your very own stamp on whatever takes your fancy!

5

Did you know?

CHOPPED SUGARS

POTATOES ARE PACKED WITH STARCH. THESE ARE POLYSUGARS (NOT SWEET AT ALL) AND CONTAIN LOTS OF ENERGY FOR YOUR CELLS. WHEN YOU EAT THEM, YOUR BODY CHOPS THEM UP LITTLE BY LITTLE INTO SIMPLER SWEET SUGARS. A HORMONE CALLED INSULIN MOVES THEM INTO YOUR CELLS.

6

> HANDS UP IF YOU'RE HAVING MASHED SPUDS FOR DINNER!

I HOPE YOU'VE GOT A LICENSE TO DRIVE THAT THING!

8

The Scotsman Patrick Bell invented the predecessor to the harvester thresher in 1826

GENTLE GIANT

When the harvest starts in July, this colossus can be seen stalking fields across the country. While farmers had to cut grain by hand in the old days, the wide cutter bars of the harvester thresher can make short work of the fields today. A threshing drum within the vehicle separates the corns from the ears and stores them in a tank. The corn is then taken to the mill by a tractor. The stalks are left on the fields to be pressed into straw bales.

Wind-driven mills have been put to good use for some 2000 years

I'VE GOT PEDAL POWER IF YOU NEED TO GET THINGS SPINNING!

CREATE

9

BY THE FORCE OF THE WIND

People have milled grain using wind power since ancient times. This force of nature drives a grinding machine, splitting the grain into its shell and core. The shells are sieved out to make wholegrain flour. This is then used by a baker to bake bread and rolls. The windmill provided the inspiration for today's wind turbines.

10

LIFE WITHOUT GRAIN IS ALMOST UNIMAGINABLE. IT GROWS IN MOST OF THE WORLD AND IS UNPARALLELED IN ITS VERSATILITY.

11

GRAIIIINS!

SWEET GRAIN

Grain comes in a variety of types, such as wheat, rye, barley and oats. Most grains have a lot in common: They're grown in the same way and all belong to the family of so-called sweet grasses. Wait, sweet?! Yes! These grains contain natural sugar called starch (which isn't sweet at all). Generally, sweet grass can always be used to bake bread.

CREATE

12

Did you know?

TRUMPETING YEAST

MOST BAKED GOODS YOU'LL FIND AT THE BAKERY ARE FLUFFY INSIDE THANKS TO A SINGLE-CELLED FUNGUS CALLED YEAST. THIS FLUFFINESS COMES FROM CO_2 - AS THE YEAST EATS THE SUGAR IN THE FLOUR, IT TRUMPETS OUT PLENTY OF GAS. FRRRT!

Barley   Wheat   Oats   Rye

13

YEAH! WHOLE-GRAIN MEANS LONGER NAPS BETWEEN MEALS!

WHOLEGRAIN LASTS

The clue is in the name – wholegrain bread is made of whole grains. These contain the unpeeled but edible shell, which includes a range of dietary fibre, vitamins, oils and minerals. The dietary fibre is particularly important in helping digestion. To have foods with more fibre in simply switch to the wholegrain version of rice, pasta or bread.

Those wholegrain rolls look terribly tasty!

HERE COMES

STANDING TALL

Look at all those stunning sunflowers in France! They can grow up to 12 feet tall, with the biggest sunflower ever grown measuring in at a whopping 30 feet! Just like the potato, they were brought here from America. Each flower head consists of 1000 to 2000 tiny five-petaled flowers. Their seeds are a vital source of food for a whole range of birds: Tits, finches, chickadees and woodpeckers to name just four.

THOSE FLOWERS WOULD MAKE A GREAT SCREEN-SAVER!

14

CREATE

15

Birds like the blue tit can't get enough of those succulent sunflower seeds!

Sunflower oil is great for frying and baking! And it's a treat for your skin, too.

On farms like this, sunflower kernels are harvested and pressed to oil

YOU'RE DARN TOOTIN' I RUN SEED THIEVES STRAIGHT OUTTA TOWN!

16

COPY THE BIRDS

Our feathered friends the birds know exactly what they're doing: Sunflower kernels contain vitamins and minerals. They're good for us, too, which is why sunflower oil is such an important product. Each year, millions of tons of seeds are grown. These are harvested in October and then pressed to extract their precious oil.

THE SUN!

FATTY FACTS!

Although healthy, sunflower seeds contain a lot of fat. And while it's true that fat is very important for helping our bodies absorb vitamins, it should be consumed cautiously. Fruits and veg have little or no fat, while oils, nuts and certain cuts of meat contain lots of it. The best fats to eat are unsaturated fats you'll find for example in fish, soy or walnuts.

Fats help the body take on vitamins, keep skin healthy and build up vital parts of our bodies

19

I CAN EVEN SOFTLY CATCH A BUTTERFLY WITH THIS MITT! I SWEAR!

Without bees and butterflies, our diet would be(e) a lot less diverse

WHY ARE FLOWERS SO BEAUTIFUL?

Ever wondered why flowers have those bright colours? They use them to attract insects like bees. These insects climb into the blossoms to slurp their sweet nectar. As they drink, a powdery substance called pollen sticks to their bodies. If the insect flies off to the next flower of the same species, it pollinates it unknowingly, helping the flower to grow fruits or seeds and, ultimately, to proliferate.

I ONCE HAD 50 BEES ON MY HEAD! TICKLY!

17

CREATE

18

SQUIRREL'S FA

I'LL CRACK THOSE NUTSHELLS WITH ONE BIG BASH!

20

GOING NUTS

Only hazelnuts, walnuts, chestnuts and macadamia belong to the family of real nuts. Surprisingly, peanuts, almonds and pistachios are not real nuts. But don't worry, these legumes, seeds and pits are bundles of energy, too. Each of them contains plenty of vitamin B, minerals and healthy fatty acids. But don't go nuts and don't eat more than a handful, as they contain loads of energy!

Nuts come in all shapes and forms

almond   hazelnut   pistachio

walnut   peanut   almond

WILL NUTS HELP ME REMEMBER MY PASS-WORD?

Walnuts almost look like tiny brains, don't they?

21

HEARTY SNACKS

Your heart is one of your most important organs: This strong muscle pumps blood throughout your system and provides your body with oxygen and the nutrients it needs. Nuts like almonds, hazelnuts, peanuts, pistachios and walnuts contain magnesium which helps to keep your heart muscles working properly. It only takes a handful of nuts each day to do the trick!

CREATE

22

SQUIRRELS USUALLY REJOICE IF THEY STUMBLE UPON A WALNUT TREE. AND THESE CUTE RODENTS AREN'T THE ONLY ONES THAT LOVE SCOFFING NUTS...

THAT NERVE NETWORK IS A FINE PIECE OF CONSTRUCTION!

23

I'M A BIG FAN OF THAT SQUIRREL'S HAIR.

GETTING ON YOUR NERVES

The body's 100 billion nerve cells are connected by even more nerve fibres in your brain. Did you know that your brain's commands are transmitted through your body as electrical impulses? If you want to walk, for instance, these tiny flashes run through the nerve fibres down to your legs. Most of these orders can be controlled. But some are beyond our control to help us survive. These are called reflexes.

24

Nerve cells look a bit like bizarre deep sea creatures

Brain teaser ①

NOW IT'S TIME TO PUT YOUR BRAIN TO THE TEST! TAKE A GOOD LOOK AT THIS BRICK FRAME FOR 15 SECONDS AND MEMORISE THE SEQUENCE OF THE COLOURS. THEN START AT BRICK 1 AND NAME ALL THE COLOURS, MOVING CLOCKWISE.*

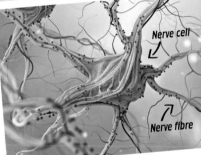

Nerve cell

Nerve fibre

Grasping is a reflex among babies

FAST, FASTER, REFLEX

Ever stumbled and wondered why you didn't come a cropper?! You may want to thank the so-called knee jerk. It's a reflex that keeps you from falling over when you stumble. By the way, there's almost no way to control reflexes as they're automatic responses to a certain stimulus. Don't believe it? Try keeping your eyes open while your mum or dad blows air into them. Say hello to the eyelid reflex!

25

ALRIGHTY, MY REFLEX IS TO GALLOP INTO THE SUNSET!

*USE YOUR OWN BRICKS AND BUILD YOUR OWN FRAMES. PLAY THE GAME "BRAIN FRAME" WITH YOUR FRIENDS OR PARENTS!

PROTEIN LIKE A

> SOME PROTEIN A DAY KEEPS THE DOCTOR AWAY!

26

27

OLD BUT GOLD

The first thing Lily and Sam learn in India is that lentils are extremely old. In fact, they're the world's oldest cultivated legume - people have been growing them for over 11,000 years! Today, they're mainly cultivated in India, come in various sizes and colours, and are very difficult to harvest. But the hard work pays off: These super tasty foods are a source of protein, minerals, dietary fibre and vitamins – at times a good substitute for meat.

> 11,000 YEARS? BETTER CHECK THE SELL-BY DATE!

PROTEIN PARTY

So what's all this buzz around protein? Well, it's essential for building, maintaining, and repairing the tissues in the body. Nothing to do with the tissues you blow your nose with, of course. Tissue cells make up most of our body: Muscles, organs, our immune system... these all largely consist of protein. So dig in and enjoy some eggs, nuts, fish, meat, soy and milk to get your fill – and don't forget the lentils!

Lentils are the great-great-great grandfathers of the food family!

Sometimes some milk keeps the doctor away – or how does that saying go?

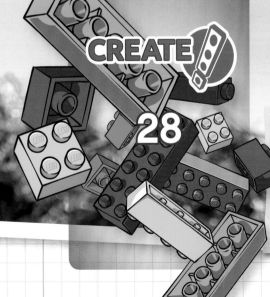

CREATE

28

NEITHER PLANT NOR ANIMAL

Move over, lentils! These are also pretty wild: Mushrooms are neither plant nor animal! These fungi grow all over the world - anywhere with enough moisture for them to feel at home. Some of them measure several square miles in size and are the biggest organisms on earth, others are tiny and even live INSIDE animals. Yikes! Though some are toxic, many mushrooms are tasty, almost fat-free and (you guessed it!) packed with protein, vitamins and minerals.

Fry them, chop them, bake them: Mushrooms are a delicacy. As well as incredibly fascinating organisms!

LILY AND SAM HAVE REACHED THE MAGICAL SUBCONTINENT OF INDIA. HERE, THEY TRACK DOWN THE OLDEST CULTIVATED LEGUME IN THE WORLD AND LEARN A WHOLE LOT ABOUT THE PUNCHY POWER OF PROTEIN.

WHAT MUSCLES DO

We have over 600 different muscles in our body – and as they mainly consist of protein, we need plenty of the stuff to build and maintain them. Muscles help us to lift things and sit upright, focus our eyes and pump blood through our body. Every muscle is made up of the same elastic material built with thousands of small fibres.

31

LET ME SHOW YOU HOW MUSCLY MY CLUBBING ARM IS...

Regular exercise and sufficient protein helps build muscles

Did you know?

SIX-LEGGED STRONG FELLOWS

SPEAKING OF MUSCLES: MEET ONE OF THE STRONGEST BEINGS ON THE ENTIRE PLANET – ANTS! THOUGH DIMINUTIVE IN SIZE, THESE LITTLE CRITTERS ARE TRUE WEIGHT-LIFTING CHAMPIONS. SOME SPECIES CAN CARRY 40 TIMES THEIR OWN WEIGHT. THEY'RE ALSO VERY HIGH IN PROTEIN. ERM, JUST SAYING...

CREATE

29

What could you carry if you could hold 40 times your own weight? A small car, no less!

30

SOUNDS LIKE THOSE ANTS SHOULD JOIN MY TEAM!

PARTNERS FOR

Anemone

Hermit crab

WOW! ALMOST AS COLOURFUL AS LEGO BRICKS!

32

COLOURFUL CAULI

This brilliant bouquet of cauliflower is edible and its colouration is completely natural. There are four different types of cauliflower - green, white, yellow and purple. Like all vegetables, this plant also contains dietary fibre.

In the 16th century, cauliflower was imported to Europe from Asia Minor

Although it could smell better, going to the toilet is not disgusting at all. Just ask this dog!

FOOD TRAVELS A LONG WAY TO REACH MY TUMMY!

33

CREATE

34

MORE FIBRE ENRICHES FOOD!

Your body can't digest dietary fibre, so why eat it at all? Well, fibre is healthy for your body in many ways. For instance, fibre provides food for your gut bacteria and helps you with digestion so you can go to the toilet regularly. Nature's calling!

WHAT DO YOU THINK CRABS AND ANEMONES OR HUMANS AND BACTERIA HAVE IN COMMON? WELL, THEY HELP FEED EACH OTHER AND OFFER MUTUAL PROTECTION AGAINST DANGEROUS ORGANISMS - EVERYONE WINS!

ME AND MY CHOPPER ARE VITAL PARTNERS, TOO!

CREATE

35

36

THEY ARE EVERYWHERE!

In 2050, there will be 10 billion people on earth. But guess what? There are about 40 trillion bacteria on and in you today! Though your first reaction might be disgust, you couldn't live without these vital partners. They help you digest your food and kill micro-organisms in your gut, mouth and skin. They feed on our food and body in return. This is called symbiosis.

In about 70 years, the world population will have more than doubled

Our bodies' bacteria have positive impact on our health

TEN BILLION IN NUMBERS: 10,000,000,000

FORTY TRILLION IN NUMBERS: 40,000,000,000,000

WORLD POPULATION

1974 4 billion
1987 5 billion
1999 6 billion
2012 7 billion
2027 8 billion (est.)
2046 9 billion (est.)

YEAR

37

I WISH I WAS AT THE BEST FEEDING GROUND – I'M STARVING

UPSTAIRS NEIGHBOUR

The hermit crab is quite happy when it has an anemone living on its shell. In fact, it even places the betentacled creature there intentionally. Why? Because this way, the crab is camouflaged and protected by the anemone's poisonous tentacles. In return, the anemone can munch some of the crab's food on the house and gets a free ride to the best feeding grounds. This is a classic symbiosis: a win-win situation.

CREATE

38

39

40

THE SWEETEST FRUITS

There's nothing quite as mouth-watering as fresh fruit! Wherever Lily and Sam travel in Asia – be it Indonesia, Thailand or Vietnam – they just can't get enough of the mangoes, papayas and passion fruits sold at local markets, on the streets or even on boats. So good, so sweet – and so healthy, too: They're packed with vitamins, antioxidants and other beneficial things and therefore make for good snacks!

Passion fruits grow on vines, mangoes grow on trees

> SWAP THIS CARROT FOR A MANGO, ANYONE?

In Asia people sell food even on boats at so-called floating markets

> TALKING OF SWEET THINGS, LET'S SING! LA LALA LALALA, OOOOH!

SO MANY SUGARS!

When we talk sugar, the powder we use to sweeten, cakes or ice cream immediately springs to mind. This is called sucrose and it's made from sugar cane or sugar beet. But it's not the only type of sugar - there's also fructose (found in fruits), glucose (honey) and lactose, a sugar found in milk and other dairy, for instance. As with everything else, sugar should only be enjoyed in moderation to stay healthy and fit.

White sugar we all use at home is made fom these plants called sugar cane

> We know, sugar tastes sooo sweet. But go easy, you're sweet enough already!

DEEP IN THE LUSH RAINFORESTS OF SOUTH-EASTERN ASIA, LILY AND SAM DISCOVER THE SWEETEST AND MOST TROPICAL FRUITS AROUND. THEY ALSO ENCOUNTER AN ANIMAL THAT JUST CAN'T GET ENOUGH OF THEM!

THIS BAT HAS STOLEN MY FRUIT! MINE, MINE MINE!!!

THE FLYING FRUIT DETECTOR

Most bats feast on a diverse diet of delicious, crunchy insects. The fruit bat (or flying fox), however, has developed a rather exclusive taste. With its sensational sense of smell, this devoted vegetarian is able to locate the ripest and sweetest fruits in the forest, so it can enjoy the most delicious pulp and nectar every time. Now gimme a bite of that mango, will ya?!

43

The flying fox is one of the largest bats. Its wing span is up to 150 cm

Spices come in every colour of the rainbow...

Did you know?

WHAT'S SALIVA GOOD FOR?

TIME FOR AN EXPERIMENT: CHEW SOME WHITE BREAD FOR AT LEAST 2 MINUTES. AFTER A WHILE, YOU'LL SUDDENLY REALISE THAT IT'S STARTED TO TASTE SWEET. THAT'S BECAUSE YOUR SALIVA BREAKS THE STARCH (A SUGAR THAT DOESN'T TASTE SWEET) INTO GLUCOSE (A SWEET SUGAR). WHAT DID WE LEARN? DIGESTION ALREADY STARTS IN YOUR MOUTH.

SPICE UP YOUR LIFE

Aaaaah, the earthy scent of cinnamon from Indonesia, the spicy taste of chilli from China, the overpowering aroma of nutmeg from Malaysia: spices are as colourful as they are fascinating! Besides, they make our food more flavourful and aromatic. Not long ago, spices were very precious goods. Luckily for us, spices are now everyday items.

AT LEAST I KNOW THESE SPICES ARE ALL GOOD!

41

CREATE

42

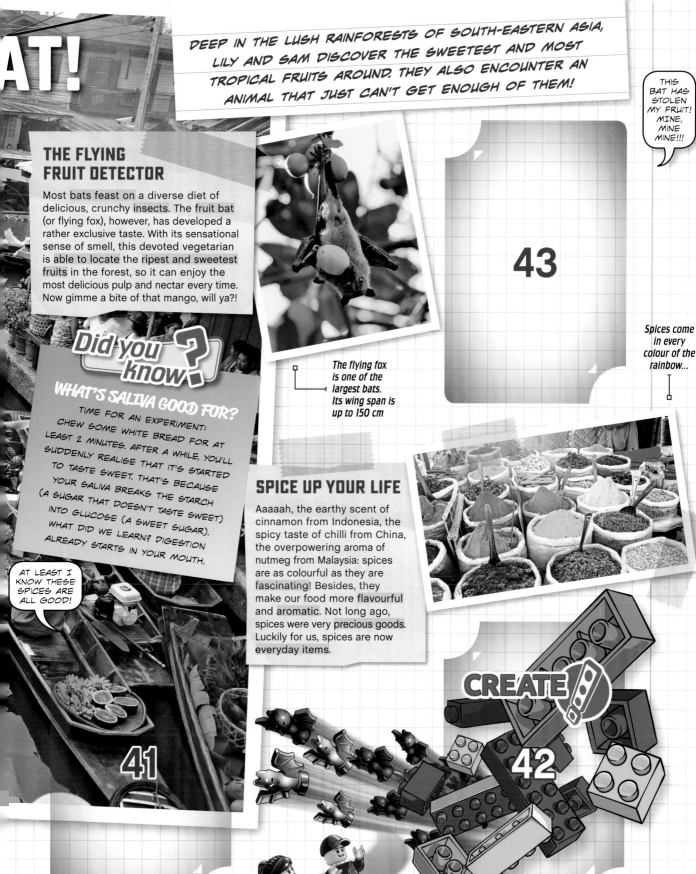

SPICE THE RICE!

Rice plants grow in watered fields like this

44

> I REMEMBER WHEN RICE WAS A NEW THING...

Rice is far from dull. It comes in a range of amazing colours

Rice noodles and spicy sauces are a well known combination in Japan

SMALL GRAIN, BIG IMPACT

Rice has been an important staple for Asian people for some 7,000 years. It's a cereal which offers up to 300 grains per plant. Besides cooking the whole grains, rice flour can also be used to make noodles or even rice paper. No, not to write on, but to make delicious wraps with veg, herbs and other delicacies. Many people love to combine the many forms of rice with soy sauce.

> I ONLY KNOW THE TASTE OF FEAR! YIKES!

45

TASTY UMAMI

Your mouth contains taste buds. You obviously know the tastes sweet, sour, bitter and salty. But have you ever heard of umami? Ingredients like soy sauce, parmesan cheese, meat, sea food or dried tomatoes can trigger the umami buds in your mouth – while mushrooms and vegetables are also rich in umami substances.

CREATE

46

I BET THAT CRAB IS LETHAL ON THE DRUMS!

47

MRS. CREEPY LEGS

Can you believe it? There's a crab in the sea around Japan with a leg span of up to 5 metres! Yet bizarrely, its body's only 38 centimetres long! But fear not, this crab looks more dangerous than it actually is: it mostly eats molluscs, plants and dead animals. To escape predators like squids, it can even disguise itself with sea sponges. Sadly this doesn't help it against fishermen, who think this giant spider crab is an umami delicacy.

48

The giant crab can grow to be 100 years old

MY TASTEBUDS SAY "GIVE ME MORE HOTDOGS!"

Did you know?

WHY WE TASTE

OUR TASTE BUDS ARE A WARNING AND DETECTION SYSTEM: SOUR OR BITTER TASTES CAN INDICATE UNRIPE, ROTTEN OR POISONOUS FOOD, WHILE SALTY, SWEET AND UMAMI HINT AT THE AMOUNT OF MINERALS OR THE CARBOHYDRATE, PROTEIN AND FAT CONTENT.

Brain teaser

SUDOKU

EVERY ROW, COLUMN AND MINI-GRID MUST CONTAIN THE NUMBERS 1 TO 4 ONLY ONCE. FIND THE SOLUTIONS ON PAGE 56!

49

NEVER EAT CRAYON. TRUST ME, IT TASTES AWFUL!

Some regions of the tongue are more sensitive for taste than others

BAAAAA OR MO

I'D DEFINITELY GO FOR "BAAAAAH"!

50

51

WE'RE OUTNUMBERED!

Australia has a population of roughly 25 million people. That's around the same as the resident cattle population, but it's nothing compared to their sheep: 75 million of these woolly souls populate this vast continent. And New Zealand even has five times as many sheep as people! Cattle and sheep are essential for remote areas: They provide the local population with meat, milk, wool and many other farming products.

Australia is home to 26 million cattle. Here are four of the best

DAIRY IS BAAAA-RILLIANT IF YOU ASK ME!

SAY CHEESE!

Milk is turned into cheese in the dairy. This is done by heating milk in large pots and adding salt, milk bacteria as well as an enzyme called rennet which separates the protein from the whey. After getting rid of most of the liquid, the cheese is then aged: Young cheese is usually mild and soft, while older ones are strong and often firm. Though there are some soft old cheeses as well. Watch out! Old cheese tends to smell a bit!

CREATE

52

No cheese without milk. And no milk without cows, sheep – or camels for that matter! There is also plant-based cheese!

)))0?

AUSTRALIA AND NEW ZEALAND ARE FULL OF SHEEP AND CATTLE. HIGH TIME, THEN, FOR LILY AND SAM TO MEET SOME VERY DILIGENT FARMERS – AND THEIR HARD-WORKING, FOUR-LEGGED STAFF.

NEW GAME – EAT ALL OF THE DELICIOUS CHEESE!

THE SECRET INGREDIENT

Making cheese from milk involves one crucial step: fermentation. This is a chemical process discovered more than 10,000 years ago to make bread, yoghurt or cheese. With cheese, it works as follows: milk bacteria are added to milk. They munch away at the milk's sugar (called lactose), produce acid to curdle the milk and turn it into creamy cheese. This is also why some cheeses seriously pong: The bacteria release stinky gasses as they work. Isn't it weird that something so delicious can be so smelly?!

Fermentation is essential for many popular foods – not least cheese!

55

Every Australian eats seven kilos of yoghurt a year. And why not? It's fermented and packed with minerals and protein!

TRICKY MINERALS

Our body needs minerals, just like it needs vitamins. The only problem is that it can't produce them itself! Macrominerals are particularly important, while trace minerals are sufficient in smaller amounts. Calcium, for instance, is a macromineral found in products like yoghurt, while iron is a trace mineral that can be found in red meat like beef. Some types of mineral water are awash with certain minerals, too.

THAT'S NO ZEBRA CROSSING – IT'S A SHEEPING POLICEMAN!

ALL THIS CHEESE! NO WONDER POLLY WANTS A CRACKER!

Brain teaser

WHICH NUMBER SHOULD REPLACE THE QUESTION MARK? WRITE YOUR ANSWER IN LEGO BRICKS!

1 2 4 7 12 20 ?

53

54

ANSWER: COMBINE THE NEIGHBOURS AND ADD 1. 1+1=2, 2+1+1=4, 4+7=11=12 … 12+20+1=33

AN APPLE A DAY

Granny Smith apple

GO, GRANNY!

Ever wondered how an apple can also be a granny? Well, easy: Like a zoologist discovers animals, Aussie woman Maria Ann Smith discovered a specific variety just outside Sydney in 1868 – and behold, the Granny Smith apple was among us! Her apple pals had been around a lot longer at this point, though: The history of this fruit goes as far back as 12,000 years! Our Granny here is famous for containing loads of chlorophyll - a dye that helps plants to use sunlight as fuel and that protects and strengthens our bodies.

MAYBE THEY'LL NAME A PEAR AFTER ME?

56

No matter the colour of an apple, they are all so healthy it's almost divine!

DON'T YOU DARE PEEL ME!

Okay, let's talk: the apple called Braeburn is an absolute smash-hit when it comes to vitamins. 100 grams of that delicious apple contain a whopping 35 mg of pure vitamin C. Still, you can't go wrong with any apple: All the good stuff is waiting right under the skin, which for instance helps to keep your heart healthy. So wash it but don't peel it, willya? Plus, there's a secret ingredient called pectin – a fibre that's great for your digestive system.

THE BIRDS AND THE BEES

Bees are not only diligently buzzing insects, they are also extremely important: By feeding on nectar and flying from flower to flower, they involuntarily carry lots of pollen around which helps plants distribute their offspring far and wide. So, there's not only no plants without bees; there'd also be next to no fruits and veggies in the supermarkets. And there would be a lot fewer apples, too.

There are fewer and fewer bees in the world – a code red!

57

BEES ARE LIKE THE COOLEST DRONES EVER!

CREATE

58

ONE BEE HOTEL COMING RIGHT UP IN A MINUTE'S TIME!

I DON'T BLAME THEM. I LIKE PRETTY FLOWERS, TOO!

An insect hotel can be a home for many bee species

Did you know?

BECOME A BFF

YOU DON'T NEED MUCH TO CREATE A BEE-FRIENDLY ENVIRONMENT IN YOUR HOME: GIVE THEM LOTS OF FLOWERS LIKE LAVENDER OR SUNFLOWERS AND PLANTS THAT YIELD FOOD ALL YEAR ROUND AND THE LITTLE BUZZERS WILL COME IN DROVES. PLUS, IF YOU HAVE THE SKILLS OF A MECHANIC, YOU CAN ALSO SEARCH ON THE INTERNET WITH YOUR PARENTS HOW TO BUILD A BEE HOTEL TO GET THE WEE INSECTS THROUGH THE WINTER.

59

60

CREATE

61

Brain teaser

LOOK AT THE SEQUENCE OF APPLES HERE. WHICH FOUR APPLES COME NEXT? SOLUTION ON PAGE 56.

GRANNY SMITH | GRANNY SMITH | BRAEBURN | GOLDEN DELICIOUS | GRANNY SMITH | GRANNY SMITH | ?

THROUGH THE

WELCOME TO THE DESERT!

The continent of Australia is many things. But above all else, it's huuuge! It's the world's sixth largest country – and the driest inhabited place on earth! No wonder: Australia is home to ten deserts, each one bigger, drier and hotter than the last. The largest of them all is the Great Victoria Desert. It's bigger than the U.K.! Although it's insanely hot and dry, it's still teeming with life: Lots of animals feel quite at home there.

I FEEL SERIOUSLY OVER-DRESSED!

62

63

THE ELIXIR OF LIFE

Though water's scarce in the desert, it is essentially the elixir of life – making up 70 percent of the earth and 50 to 60 percent of our bodies! Water makes plants grow and our blood flow, allows us to sweat to regulate body temperature, makes our cells work and washes toxic substances out of our system (through you know what!). Without water, our bodies would shut down after a few days. So stay hydrated and always drink enough water. 2 to 3 litres a day are a healthy amount for a grown-up.

Kangaroos only live in Australia!

I'M GONNA NEED A NEW JOB!

Without water, the entire planet would be a desert

CREATE

64

The thorny devil doesn't look for water – water looks for him!

SURVIVAL OF THE THORNIEST

This lizard is a peculiar fellow and a proper hero: The thorny devil is one of the longest-living lizards on earth, living for 20 or more years. It's also a true genius when it comes to surviving in the dry desert. It simply condenses water on its spiky armour. All those spikes are designed to catch dew or rain, and transport it straight to the lizard's mouth. Clever little devil!

DESERT!

Watch out! Kangaroos are wild animals and could cross the road at any given time

> DEHYDRATION DEFINITELY ISN'T FUNNY!

67

Average adults carry roughly five litres of blood in their bodies. It's made of blood cells like these here

Did you know?

THE SALT WATER PARADOX!

STRANGE BUT TRUE: THE MORE SALT WATER YOU DRINK, THE MORE THIRSTY YOU'LL BECOME. WHY? WELL, OUR BRAIN KNOWS EXACTLY HOW MUCH SALT IS TOO MUCH FOR US. THE MORE SALTY BRINE WE CHUG, THE MORE IT SIGNALS FOR US TO KEEP DRINKING WATER TO BALANCE OUT THE AMOUNT OF SALT WE'RE CONSUMING. DRINKING TOO MUCH SALT WATER CAN EVEN BE DANGEROUS AS THE SALT DRAINS THE WATER FROM OUR CELLS AND DRIES THEM OUT. YIKES!

Saltwater crocodiles have special organs designed to get rid of the salt in the sea water

IT'S IN THE BLOOD!

Blood is essentially what keeps us alive. With every heartbeat, blood rushes through us, transporting oxygen and nutrients to all parts of the body to make our cells work. Blood also fights infections to help you get well quickly. It's made up of plasma as well as red and white blood cells. If you want to help your body increase its circulation of blood, reach for some onions. You might need lots of them to make it work – but your blood will be running just fine!

65

66

> MAYBE THE ONIONS WILL SCARE THE DOG AWAY, TOO!

> THIS PLACE NEEDS WATERMELON DUDE – EMPHASIS ON THE WATER!

ON THE MOVE!

A SUCCESS STORY ON TWO LEGS

Can you imagine that walking upright is a direct consequence of climate change? True story: As forests receded and savannah started to spread out our early ancestors had to adapt to new forms of foraging and hunting, often meaning they had to walk great distances. This is way more effectively and comfortably done on two legs rather than four. Walking upright also meant they could see further and spot enemies or prey earlier. And with their hands free, they were better hunters or cooks. Classic win-win situation.

I'M THE NEXT STEP IN HUMAN EVOLUTION!

68

It's been a whopping 7,5 million years since man slowly began walking upright

No weekends in sight: Early man was constantly perfecting and refining his sharp and pointy weapons

IT'S ALL ABOUT THE BALANCE!

Cutlery? Not yet invented! A grocery store around the corner? Nope! Early humans collected and hunted their food and used sharp stones to get meat off the bones. In the beginning, our earliest ancestors fed on carcasses while later successors went hunting and prepared their meals over a fire. Plants, roots and berries were also an integral part of their diet, giving a relatively good balance that supported the evolution and helped them stay healthy.

I LOVE THAT ANCIENT CUTLERY! SOOO RUSTIC!

69

CREATE

70

Australopithecus is one of our oldest extinct ancestors

FIND ME AN OSTRICH — I WANT A PROPER RACE!

I'VE RUSTLED UP A DELICIOUS BOWL OF ENERGY!

READY, SET, GO!

Whoever runs fastest or endures longest wins. That was the case even back then when our ancestors started walking upright. They didn't run races, of course: They ran to hunt down animals with spears or stones. They also ran to survive the attack of an ill-tempered sabretooth tiger. And that was even more important than getting a medal at the finish line.

71

72

All foods contain energy, some more than others!

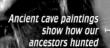
Ancient cave paintings show how our ancestors hunted

TALKING ABOUT ENERGY

Laughing, running, playing with LEGO bricks, even brushing your teeth: everything you do burns energy. We refuel energy by eating and drinking. Many athletes consume foods like whole-grain noodles or potatoes before their training or upcoming event. That's because they contain carbohydrates, which are excellent at providing energy for the body.

ON AND ON AND ON AND...

Our ancestors were tough work horses when it came to running. They may not have been the fastest ones around but they simply ran on and on and on. In fact, they kept chasing their prey for so long it eventually dropped of exhaustion. This useful talent is courtesy of our physique: Short toes for better walking, little hair and lots of perspiratory glands preventing the body from overheating and long legs for long strides. In fact, our feet are similar to those of the ostrich: Long shanks, high thighs are perfect for running fast and long.

An ostrich can speed at up to 44 miles per hour for a long time: He outruns humans easily

73

MY AWESOME RHYMES JUST DON'T STOP EITHER!

IT'S GETTING H

74

75

I LIKE PLAYING DRESS UP, BUT IT'D BE STUPID TO PLAY WITH REAL FIRE-WORKS!

THE TAMING OF THE FLAME

Nobody knows exactly when and where humans first made fire. But one thing is for sure: it changed the course of history! Suddenly, our ancestors were able to ward off animals, keep warm and heat their food - all of which brought unforeseen advantages. Evidence suggests that this goes back as far as 400,000 years. Perhaps it all started with a forest fire or a lightning strike. Further down the line, our ancestors then learned to use flint and other tools to make fire at will.

Controlling fire was one of the most important discoveries humankind ever made!

I HEART FIRE – UNCOOKED PIZZA IS INEDIBLE!

Cooking food is still a big thing today

CREATE

76

Brain teaser

MATCHES ARE GREAT FOR STARTING A FIRE. WHICH MATCHES HAVE TO MOVE FOR THE SUM BELOW TO BE CORRECT? FIND THE SOLUTION ON PAGE 56!

$$1 + 2 = 8$$

ALWAYS ASK AN ADULT BEFORE USING MATCHES!

HEAT IT UP!

As soon as humankind learned to control fire and heat food with it, we made a huge evolutionary leap: Heating food made it easier and safer for certain foods to be consumed, which in turn meant that foods could be eaten more easily and new foods could become part of the diet –improving the overall diet quality. It also killed a lot of bacteria and parasites, and paved the way for countless new foods – our ancestors could suddenly enjoy roots that were inedible or even toxic when raw.

AS LILY AND SAM CONTINUE THEIR TRAVELS THROUGH AFRICA WITH ITS MAJESTIC GRASSLANDS AND VAST DESERTS, THEY LEARN A LOT ABOUT AN EXTREMELY IMPORTANT ELEMENT — FIRE.

CREATE

79

Wildfires are dangerous for humans and animals

FUELLED BY FIRE

Forest fires are devastating and dangerous. But in some regions on earth they're also very important – provided they're not man-made but naturally occurring. Natural wildfires play a vital role in nature. Burning dead wood or brush releases otherwise trapped nutrients back into the soil where they can encourage new growth. Wildfires can also rid an area of diseased plants and harmful insects.

The lion, strong as it may be, is wary of fire

OK, NO FIRE, BUT I STILL NEED SCENTED CANDLES!

77

78

SET THAT FIRE AND KEEP MY SHOWER WATER HOT!

FEAR OF FIRE

Most animals fear fire. They shy away from it instinctively – even if they've never been burned by it. There are plenty of reasons for this: Many animals don't like bright light, and they can also sense the heat of a fire and the smell of smoke from far away. Their instincts tell them that fire can burn them, hurt them and destroy their home. Setting campfires allowed early humans to protect themselves against wild beasts effectively.

FULL THROTT

I'M PACKING SOME SORGHUM BEFORE BLASTING OFF!

80

DRY AND HOT

Africa is a magnificent and exciting continent. In some parts of Africa the weather is extremely dry and hot which can make it difficult for some fruits and veggies to grow. A strong, resilient grain like sorghum, however, is able to grow in warm and dry conditions. Consequently, it's one of Africa's staple foods – and a healthy one at that: Sorghum is rich in nutrients. The grains contain mainly starch and also fibre as well as other vitamins and minerals.

Sorghum (left) is an important crop in Africa. Some tasty couscous dishes (right) use it as a base

WHAT'S THE BIGGEST MUSCLE? I'LL GET TO THE BOTTOM OF IT!

BODY'S POWER PLANTS

Did you know that you have ca. 640 skeletal muscles in your body? It's true: The smallest of them all is right in your ear, the biggest is what you're sitting on right now. You know what we're talking about! No matter where: Every single muscle needs energy to function the way you want it to. To store and use energy found in nutrients, muscles and all other cells need molecules called ATP (adenosine triphosphate). They're found in little cell compartments called mitochondria – these are essentially tiny batteries.

I USE 600 MUSCLES FINDING MY JAMMIES!

81

82

Certain foods and some exercise will help make your muscles grow bigger

OUR MUSCLES CONTAIN MITOCHONDRIAL POWER PLANTS THAT GIVE THE MUSCLES THE POWER TO RUN AND HELP KEEP US WARM. THEY WORK 24/7 AND NEED LOTS OF ENERGY TO FUNCTION PROPERLY.

THE PERFECT PREDATOR

Now, as much energy as our muscles may have available to use, no human on this planet is faster than sprinter Usain Bolt, clocking in at 27 miles per hour over a very short distance. Cheetahs, however, the fastest animals on land, can accelerate up to 75 miles per hour – thanks to a slim body, muscular legs, flexible spine and powerful claws! That long tail even allows them to abruptly change direction at top speed.

CREATE

84

83

MITOCHONDRIA? NITRO-CHONDRIA, MORE LIKE!

Mitochondria are our very own eco power plants to keep us going!

Did you know?

FOR A BRIGHT FUTURE

YOU DO NOT NEED TO BUY SORGHUM OR OTHER PRODUCTS MADE ON OTHER CONTINENTS. MANY SIMILAR OR EVEN IDENTICAL PRODUCTS ARE GROWN IN EUROPE, TOO. YOU CAN HELP THE ENVIRONMENT SIMPLY BY KEEPING AN EYE ON WHERE YOUR GROCERY SHOPPING COMES FROM. OFTEN THE NEARER THE FOOD IS PRODUCED THE BETTER IT IS FOR THE ENVIRONMENT. FOOD LABELS WILL SHOW THIS. THAT WAY YOU CAN EASILY EAT A SUSTAINABLE DIET.

A cheetah accelerates faster than a Ferrari!

85

SHOULD I STOP GETTING MY SPROUTS FROM MARS?

FULL POWER!

Everything you eat feeds your body with important nutrients. They are carried to the cells via the bloodstream. In our cells, tiny power stations are doing their meticulous work – they are called mitochondria. They play an important role in converting nutrients into pure energy and function best when they have plenty of oxygen to work with. Once new energy is produced, you can run ahead with renewed power – like a freshly charged mobile phone.

UNDER

I WON'T NEED TO EXAGGERATE ANY MORE!

THE GREAT WHITE SHARK

The waters around South Africa are home to a world-famous beast: The great white shark! A fearsome fish for many, this perfect predator has over 300 razor-sharp teeth between its jaws! However, it doesn't quite deserve its reputation as a vile and murderous beast: in fact, it's not at all interested in humans. Luckily for us, as the largest sharks can measure up to 20 feet in length! Its streamlined shape and powerful fins allow it to shoot through the water at a whopping 37 miles per hour!

300 RAZOR-SHARP TEETH?! I'M OUTTA HERE!

86

87

PLENTY OF FISH

South Africa's coastal waters are abundant with fish and various other creatures of the deep. This, combined with the pleasant weather and numerous natural wonders, makes South Africa a favourite destination for amateur anglers from all over the world. Despite modern technology, traditional fishing is still popular in South Africa, with many people committed to preserving the natural balance and unique wildlife found around the nation's 3,000 kilometres of coastline.

Fishermen head out to sea every day with these little boats

The Great White Shark feels quite at home along South Africa's coasts

CREATE

88

Brain teaser

SOMETHING FISHY

LOOK AT THESE TWO PICTURES. CAN YOU SPOT FIVE DIFFERENCES? YOU CAN CHECK FOR THE ANSWERS ON PAGE 56.

COPY

ORIGINAL

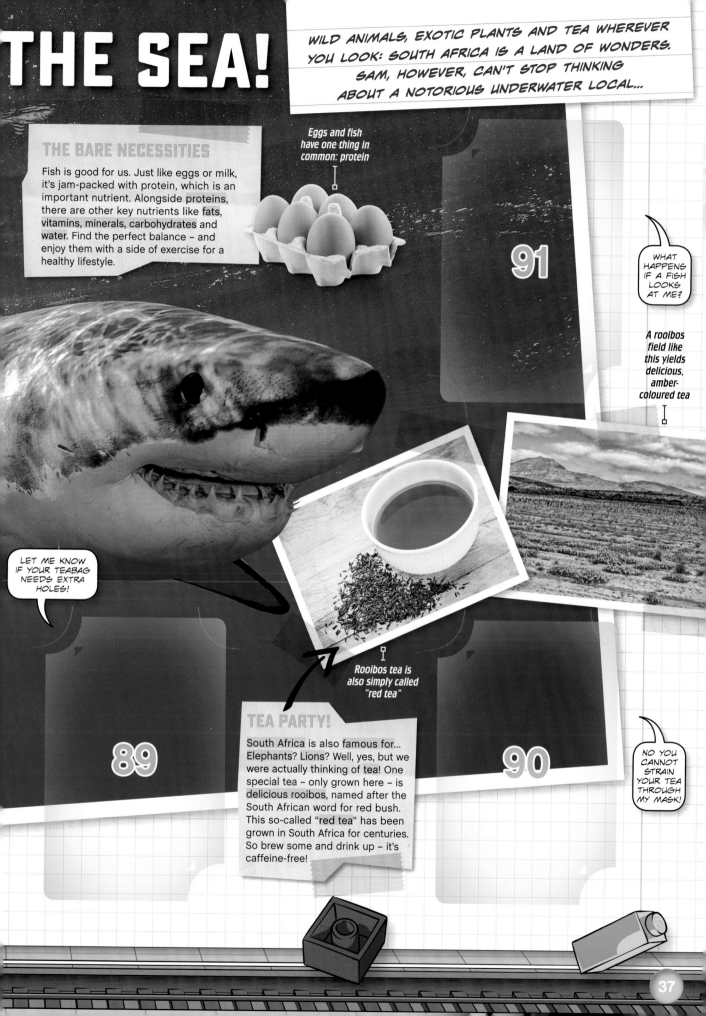

THE SEA!

THE BARE NECESSITIES

Fish is good for us. Just like eggs or milk, it's jam-packed with protein, which is an important nutrient. Alongside proteins, there are other key nutrients like fats, vitamins, minerals, carbohydrates and water. Find the perfect balance – and enjoy them with a side of exercise for a healthy lifestyle.

Eggs and fish have one thing in common: protein

91

WHAT HAPPENS IF A FISH LOOKS AT ME?

A rooibos field like this yields delicious, amber-coloured tea

LET ME KNOW IF YOUR TEABAG NEEDS EXTRA HOLES!

Rooibos tea is also simply called "red tea"

89

TEA PARTY!

South Africa is also famous for... Elephants? Lions? Well, yes, but we were actually thinking of tea! One special tea – only grown here – is delicious rooibos, named after the South African word for red bush. This so-called "red tea" has been grown in South Africa for centuries. So brew some and drink up – it's caffeine-free!

90

NO YOU CANNOT STRAIN YOUR TEA THROUGH MY MASK!

SWIMMING EL[

Sea elephants can weigh up to 4 tonnes – no less than four compact cars

92

DO YOU THINK I'LL FIND A SNOWBOW DOWN HERE?

TOPIC: BODY HEAT

When travelling in countries where temperatures can get very low, physical activities like walking may require more energy. Reasons for that could be heavier clothing or having to walk through piles of snow. That's why Arctic explorers on an expedition need more energy per day to keep their bodies going, depending on the level of physical activity. Of course the right clothing is vital, too. Wearing several layers of clothes can keep you cosy and warm. Without clothes no one can survive a day in the Antarctic.

Need to keep warm? Try layering!

Pretty warm – inside an igloo it's up to 15° Celsius

I STILL REGRET NOT BRINGING SLIPPERS!

93

Did you know?

HOUSES MADE OF SNOW

YOU ARE SEEKING REFUGE FROM CHILLING TEMPERATURES IN A HOUSE MADE OF SNOW? ACTUALLY A GREAT IDEA! ALTHOUGH IT LOOKS A BIT FROSTY, THE AIR TRAPPED INSIDE THE SNOW WALLS IS PRETTY GOOD INSULATION. IF YOU WARM UP THE INSIDE WITH YOUR OWN BODY HEAT, THE WARMTH CAN'T BREAK OUT AND THE COLD CAN'T ENTER. BUT BETTER BE CAREFUL: YOU NEED TO RENEW THE WALLS IF YOU DON'T WANT YOUR IGLOO TO MELT OVER YOUR HEAD.

CREATE

94

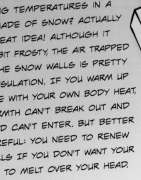

WELCOME TO ANTARCTICA, HOME OF THE SEA ELEPHANT. SAM AND LILY NEED TO WEAR 5 LAYERS OF CLOTHING AND HAVE SOME EXTRA FOOD TO STAY WARM ON THIS CONTINENT.

THIS DOESN'T MAKE ME LOOK TOO MUCH LIKE A SQUID, DOES IT?

SEA ELEPHANTS' ICE BATH

Taking a bath in the icy antarctic sea might not be a good idea – unless you're a Southern Sea Elephant. Those guys don't even blink an eye when they dive into bone-chilling water to hunt for squids, rays, eels and even small sharks. While these biggest of all seals are in the water for up to two hours they're well protected against freezing to death by a mighty layer of brown fat.

CREATE

95

96

A sea elephant pup playing merrily in ice-cold water

FAT AS A HEATER

Our bodies contain tissue made up of fat which acts as an important energy store and also keeps us warm. But have you ever heard of brown fat? Unlike white fat, which is mainly an energy store, brown fat can produce heat by chemical reactions in the fat cells. Lots of animals living in cold regions do have high amounts of brown fat. Human babies are also born with brown fat to help them keep warm, but as we grow up, we normally do not have much brown fat any more.

Although babies have brown fat cells, they need to be kept warm by clothing, too

Brain teaser

Snow petrel

Weddell seal

Start

ICY MAZE

IT'S FREEZING OUTSIDE! CAN YOU FIND THESE ANTARCTIC ANIMALS A WAY INTO THE COZY WARMTH OF THE IGLOO? FIND THE SOLUTION ON PAGE 56.

End

97

THE COLD AIR IS UNDER ARREST – FOR STEALING MY BREATH!

Ross seal

Emperor penguin

98

99

IT'S LIKE A FAMILY REUNION!

Chimoyas and guavas are just two of countless super tasty South American fruits!

TIME TO GO BANANAS!

Throughout the trip, Sam's been looking forward to finally getting the lowdown on bananas. First he learns that these delicious treats don't grow from seeds but from bulbs. Incredibly, they're actually berries! The fruits are harvested on huge plantations while still green some nine to twelve months after sowing. Unlike many other fruits, bananas grow all year round, allowing us to enjoy them non-stop. And this we should: They are a good source of the vital mineral potassium.

Banana plants are often mistaken for trees. In fact, they're herbs!

THE THING ABOUT VITAMINS

We've been talking about vitamins quite a lot lately, haven't we? High time then to discuss what these tiny molecules do for us: Like minerals, vitamins are nutrients that help our body work the way it's supposed to – they boost the immune system, support growth and help cells do their job. You can get your vitamins from the foods you eat every day. Many fruits, like apples, are packed with vital vitamins.

WOULD YOU LIKE YOUR FRUIT CUBED OR SLICED? HIII-YA!

Our immune system does everything to protect us from harm

CREATE

100

THE KNIGHTS PATROLLING OUR BODIES

The better our immune system, the faster we can usually recover after illness. Essentially, our immune system consists of a whole host of single proteins, cells and organs working together to protect us and tackle viruses, bacteria or other intruders. We can boost our immune system with vitamins from fruits and veggies for example, by getting enough sleep and treating it to exercise. Your knight will thank you for it!

BANANA

CREATE!

103

> SHOO, PESKY BACTERIA, BEFORE I GET MEDIEVAL ON YOU!

DOCTOR NATURE

Nature is like one big medicine cabinet – with a tree, plant, flower or herb for almost every ailment. In fact, many plants have been used as medicine for thousands of years: 25 percent of medicines we have today, like painkillers or cough syrup, are originally derived from plants! That's astonishing considering less than five percent of the plants found around the Amazon have been studied for health benefits to date.

This little guy lives in Brazil, Bolivia and Peru

101

ANIMALS AS DOCTORS

A lot of animals are able to self-medicate. Elephants, birds, bees and bonobos have all been observed eating things that make them feel better, prevent disease, or kill parasites and viruses. Bonobos, for instance, swallow bundles of liana leaves to get rid of parasites and heal the wounds they cause. Moustache tamarins swallow large seeds to do the same. No vets needed here!

102

> YOU GET A LOLLYPOP AND A STICKER FROM ME, THOUGH!

*A manioc corm c
grow over 3 feet*

WE FOUND THE BIGGEST POTATO ON EARTH! OH, IT'S MANIOC YOU SAY?!

104

You can grind manioc to flour or make chips and even crisps from it

STEP ASIDE, POTATO

Manioc is poisonous!? Brace yourself, it's perfectly edible when cooked or fried. The manioc corm, sometimes also called yuca or cassava, is white on the inside and brown on the outside. It's rich in starch and a staple for many people around the world. One could call the manioc the South American potato – but way bigger. Imagine a potato the size of a 20 lb basketball! Wow!

CAN I CHECK YOUR MANIOC'S PASSPORT, PLEASE?

105

CREATE

106

ROOT AROUND THE WORLD

While the manioc's roots are based in tropical South America – get it? – today it's cultivated in Asia and Africa as well. Thanks to Portuguese explorers, it came to Africa's west coast. That's a distance of around 3,800 miles! Quite a dangerous journey for a little plant back in the 16th century! Today Nigeria is even the biggest cultivator of manioc worldwide. 500 million people around the world use it as staple food nowadays. Bon appetit!

SAM AND LILY ARE IN BRAZIL, HOME OF MANIOC AND COCOA. TIME FOR A FUNNY SOUNDING DRINK CALLED XOCOLATL IN THEIR GLASSES AND SOME BIG TUBEROUS ROOTS ON THEIR PLATES.

COCOA RUGBY

The shape of a cocoa fruit reminds us of a rugby ball. Though it would probably look ridiculous to use it in a real match! But let's not get off topic! Cocoa beans are actually way too bitter to be eaten right away. So after cutting the fruit off the tree and extracting the cocoa beans, they get soaked with water and stored for quite some time in banana leaves. This way they lose their bitter taste and develop the well-known cocoa flavour. In this process they also change colour from a whiteish-yellow to brown. Finally they are dried, the fermentation is complete and you have raw cocoa ready for your birthday cake, for example!

107

108

CAN WE PLAY PIN THE TAIL ON THE XOCOLATL?

AND NOW I LOVE COCOA EVEN MORE!

After the fermentation process, cocoa still tastes a bit bitter

Did you know?

CHOCOLATE ORIGINS

"XOCOLATL" OR "CHOCOL HAA" SOUND AMAZING AND STRANGE! ACTUALLY THIS IS THE SOURCE FROM WHICH THE WORD CHOCOLATE IS DERIVED. BUT IT TASTES NOTHING LIKE THE STUFF MANY PEOPLE LOVE SO MUCH! THIS MIXTURE OF WATER AND COCOA POWDER TASTES VERY BITTER. THE ANCIENT AZTECS AND MAYANS WERE KNOWN ENTHUSIASTS OF THIS DRINK. AS EUROPEANS HAD A HARD TIME PRONOUNCING THE WORD THEY CAME UP WITH THE EASIER BUT WRONG PRONUNCIATION "CHOCOLATE". THE REST IS HISTORY.

Brain teaser

FIND THE COCOA FRUITS

COCOA FRUITS HAVE BEEN SCATTERED ALL AROUND THESE TWO PAGES, CAN YOU FINDE THEM ALL? ADD THE TWO ONES RIGHT HERE ABOVE! FIND THE SOLUTION ON PAGE 56.

CREATE

109

GREEN GOLD

The avocado is one of the most important products of Peru. It's super healthy, super tasty – and actually a berry! Buckle up: Many vitamins and minerals hide under its skin! And that's not all: Avocados have lots of unsaturated fats which are good for our hearts. Unsaturated fats are liquid at room temperature and have one or more double bonds between its molecules. These fats are considered healthier than saturated fats. Those are solid at room temperature and only have single bonds between their molecules.

110

111

WONDERFUL FLAVOUR AND HEALTHY? OUI, OUI, OUI!

Unsaturated fats help protect our hearts and keep them healthy

AVOCADO PIT YOU SAY? LOOKS LIKE AN ASTEROID!

A simple trick lets you grow an avocado tree in your home

GROW YOUR OWN!

Peru is one of the world's biggest producers of avocados. However, you don't have to fly all the way to South America to see a real avocado tree. All you have to do is enjoy an avocado, wash and dry the pit afterwards, fill a jar with water and put in the pit with the broad end facing down. Press three toothpicks around the pit to stop it from falling in. Place the jar in a warm, sunny spot, but out of direct sunlight. Top up water as needed and watch your pit sprout roots and a stem after a couple of weeks. Put it in a pot with soil. A-WOW-cado!

CREATE

112

Brain teaser

LOOK AT THE SEQUENCE OF BRICKS. FIGURE OUT WHICH BRICK HAS TO BE AT THE END! FIND THE SOLUTION ON PAGE 56.

A)

B)

C)

D)

E)

AVOCADOS

Llamas are the true celebrities of Peru!

CREATE 115

Alpacas are the smallest members of the camel family

HEY LLAMA! DON'T YOU DARE TO SPIT OUT MY FUSE, WILLYA!?

SPIT IT OUT!

If there is something like a heraldic animal in South American Peru, it's most definitely the extra awesome llama! Part of the family of camels, llamas are in fact the oldest domesticated animals in the world! They were mainly used for transportation and are very social creatures. If they are agitated, however, they tend to spit with an impressive aim. Better watch out!

FLUFFY ALPACAS AHEAD!

Alpacas are even more fluffy and cuddly! They are related to the llamas but not the same species. They give more wool than llamas, too – a good thing for the Peruvians, what with alpaca wool being worth more than llama wool. Roughly 3.5 million charming alpacas are hopping around Peru and the Andes, growing fleece that's extremely soft, warm and durable. Some people think it's not the best idea to buy alpaca clothing, though, because animals can be harmed during shearing.

113

114

I TRIED HARD TO GROW MYSELF ALPACA FUR!

Make sure you buy fair-trade & harm-free alpaca clothing only!

SURE AS EGGS

LIKE A KING

Why is having a good breakfast a good idea? Your body needs plenty of good energy to get through the day. Being hangry in school is not the best way to get along with your classmates and teachers. Your brain won't like having to think about maths either, if it's out of fuel. To kickstart your body in the morning it's good to give it all the essential nutrients and you can bet: Eggs can help you achieve exactly that.

MRS. HEN, MAY I BORROW A BOILED EGG FOR MY PRETZEL?

116

FUEL IN A SHELL

Ever tried to squash a raw egg in your fist without using your thumb? Well you won't succeed! Its contents are so precious, nature has equipped this little thingie with an extremely solid shell. Eggs are rich in good protein, fats, minerals and vitamins. Add some wholegrain bread and a warm rooibos tea and you have everything to start the day well!

BLAST-O-DERM SOUNDS LIKE A MUST-HAVE TO ME!

117

Air cell
Albumen
Yolk
Germinal disc (blastoderm)
Chalazae
Shell

Anatomy of an egg

118

EASTER BUNNY

You can't beat a chocolate egg hunt at Easter. Build a nice little surprise for one of your friends and hide it somewhere for them to find!

MY FLAMINGO ONLY LAYS ONE EGG A YEAR!

119

MEGA EGG

Riddle: Your task is to prepare breakfast for 25 people, but you only have one egg to serve. How in the world can you manage to share it fairly? No problem at all: Just make sure it's an ostrich egg. It weighs over 3 lb, is up to 6 inches long and 25 times bigger than a hen's egg. But check you have a drill handy! The shell is extremely thick and rock solid!

120

THIS OSTRICH EGG IS AS MEGA AS MY BOOM BOX!

I ostrich egg and 10 hens' eggs

The ostrich is the biggest bird on earth with the biggest eggs

Did you know?

WHAT IS VEGAN?

SOME PEOPLE DON'T WANT TO INTEFERE WITH ANIMALS' LIVES AT ALL. THEY DON'T EAT DAIRY PRODUCTS, EGGS OR HONEY OR ANYTHING MADE FROM OR BY ANIMALS. IF YOU'RE STRICTLY VEGAN YOU MIGHT ALSO BE AGAINST SHOES OR BAGS MADE FROM LEATHER. MOST VEGANS KNOW EXACTLY WHAT TO EAT TO STAY HEALTHY: ALL SORTS OF VEGGIES, FRUITS, MUSHROOMS AND GRAIN WILL JUST DO FINE! THERE'S ONE VITAL VITAMIN THAT NEEDS TO BE SUBSTITUTED WITH AN ARTIFICIAL VERSION, THOUGH: VITAMIN B12. IT IS MOSTLY FOUND IN ANIMAL PRODUCTS BUT HARDLY AT ALL IN PLANTS OR FUNGHI.

NO MEAT ON THE TABLE!

There are people who don't want to eat animals for different reasons: Some love animals so much they don't want to harm them. Others do it for environmental or health reasons. Some just don't like the taste of meat. Some do it for all the above. If vegetarians substitute meat with eggs, cheese and loads of vegetables, fruits and nuts, it sure is a healthy way of living. More and more people are completely or at least mostly vegetarian.

CREATE

121

If you're vegetarian your breakfast could look like this

VEGGIE OR GRAIN?

In The United States, no barbecue is complete without some grilled corn! It's a super popular cross between veggie and grain that actually belongs to the family of grasses (as you already know) and is grown in huge fields in North America. In fact, the USA is the biggest corn (or maize) producer in the whole world – they even have an area called the "corn belt". In the days of the early settlers, corn was so valuable in North America that it was used as money and traded for other products.

CREATE

123

122

> THEY DO WHAT WITH THEIR CORN?

So popular: With the exception of Antarctica, every continent on earth produces corn!

Corn in very different colours has been grown for thousands of years

CORN FLAKES AND MORE

Corn comes in countless varieties and colours. It can be eaten directly from the cob and is also added to many foods such as cereals (corn flakes!), soups and even chewing gum. There's even a sugar that can be extracted from it. In its most natural and unprocessed form, it's rich in fibre, vitamins and minerals and can benefit your health. However, be careful not to add too much sugar to your cornflakes, as this sugar can increase the chance of illnesses like diabetes or obesity.

124

> CHOP CHOP, I NEED THAT POPCORN ASAP!

POP! POP! POP!

One of the most delicious ways to process corn is by turning it into natural popcorn (without added sugar of course)! But how the heck does it pop? The answer to that lies in the water: Inside each kernel of corn is a wee droplet of water surrounded by a shell that is called a hull. If you heat the corn, the water turns into steam, and the steam builds pressure inside the kernel. At some point, the hull can't contain the pressure any longer and goes... POP!

At the cinema it's best to take your popcorn slightly salted!

CORN!

THAT CORN WILL BE LOVELY IN MY CAULDRON CASSEROLE!

127

Corn cobs are a firm favourite of birds, too

Brain teaser

IN THIS GRID YOU CAN FIND FIVE HIDDEN WORDS!

```
K X Z A M E R I C A
Y Z S A L T Y G N C W
D E L I C I O U S X
Q F P Q Y M D C B R
S R O Z X O L Z M B
L W P Z J J V L X S M
T X C K Z I J Q K T
F M O Y Q E H D X C
Y K R J P S X X T X
X H N W V X W Z Z T
```

FIND THE SOLUTIONS ON PAGE 56.

SWEET, SWEETER, CORN

In total, there are seven different types of corn out there, each with their specific fields of use: Dent corn, flint corn, pod corn, popcorn, flour corn, waxy corn and sweetcorn. Sweetcorn is – you guessed right! – sweeter than other corn and popular all around the globe. Fresh, canned, frozen or squashed to mash: In North America, almost no veggie is more popular than sweetcorn.

125

CREATE

126

I THINK I'M ADDICTED TO CORN, TOO!

SAM AND LILY MADE IT TO MEXICO AND HAVE ALREADY DISCOVERED THE HOTTEST PLANT THERE IS: CHILLI PEPPER! THESE ARE SO HOT THEY CAN MAKE ANYONE TEAR UP. BUCKLE UP, SAM AND LILY ARE IN FOR A HOT RIDE!

LIKE

128

I THINK I'LL HAVE A LITTLE RED FACE AFTER THIS CHILLI!

HOOOOT!!!

Mexico is one of the countries which is famous for its spicy food. But why would anyone eat hot food when it's hot outside anyway? One of the compounds in chilli peppers is called capsaicin. It is the reason why our mouth burns and what makes us sweat. As sweating helps the human body cool down, it is thought that this may be the reason hot chilli peppers are so popular in hot countries. There you go: Chilli peppers help you to keep cool.

ATTENTION: SPICY!

Chilli peppers can be pretty hot. But why? That's actually pretty simple. In order to not get eaten by every passing animal, these peppers developed a defence mechanism – the spiciness. Funnily enough, most peppers are eaten exactly because of their spiciness – well, that didn't work out. By the way, the Carolina Reaper holds the record for the hottest pepper in the world. A truly fitting name!

Capsaicin hides in the seeds and the white parts inside the pepper

SCOVILLE SCALE

PURE CAPSAICIN	15,000,000
PEPPER SPRAY	2,000,000 - 5,300,000
CAROLINA REAPER	1,400,000 - 2,200,000
TRINIDAD SCORPION	1,200,000 - 2,000,000
GHOST PEPPER	855,000 - 1,041,427
CHOCOLATE HABANERO	425,000 - 577,000
SAVINA HABANERO	350,000 - 577,000
FATALI	125,000 - 325,000
HABANERO	100,000 - 350,000
SCOTCH BONNET	100,000 - 350,000
THAI	50,000 - 100,000
CAYENNE	30,000 - 50,000
TABASCO	30,000 - 50,000
SERRANO	10,000 - 23,000
HUNGARIAN	5,000 - 10,000
JALAPENO	2,500 - 8,000
POBLANO	1,000 - 1,500
ANAHEIM	500 - 2,500
PIMIENTO	100 - 500
BELL PEPPER	0

CREATE

130

129

STEP AWAY FROM THE CHILLI, STEP AWAY FROM THE CHILLI!

Did you know?

SCOVILLE SCALE

TO MEASURE THE SPICINESS THE SCOVILLE SCALE WAS INVENTED, WHICH DIRECTLY MEASURES HEAT. THE HIGHER THE SCOVILLE SCORE THE HOTTER THE PEPPER AND THE MORE CAPSAICIN IT CONTAINS.

131

HEY TREE, TALK TO ME!

Did you know that plants can communicate? It's not like they can talk to you – unless you're Flower Pot Girl. Plants use chemical reactions to communicate with other plants. The Mimosa tree is the perfect example. If this tree gets attacked by a swarm of hungry insects, it starts to release an odour-free gas. Other Mimosa trees around react to the gas immediately: they concentrate tanning agents in their leaves to make them unedibly bitter. Disgusted insects, happy Mimosa!

132

MY COFFEE'S ONLY BITTER IF THAT'S HOW YOU LIKE IT!

Listen closely: plants can communicate with each other

Some cacti are edible. They taste a bit like a bitter version of a cucumber.

HOW WOULD YOU LIKE YOUR CACTUS?

Imagine stepping on a cactus. Yikes – that hurts! Hard to believe that these spiky plants are edible and even healthy! Well, at least some of them if prepared correctly. Don't go around biting into cactus plants! Recently the cactus has become really popular in kitchens all around the world – especially in Mexico. They can be used for lots of different foods, and some are even used in smoothies!

WOW, CACTUS SOUNDS LIKE A BIG HIT! I CAN RELATE!

SPIKE LEAF

A cactus has no leaves? Sorry, you're wrong! It has plenty! It's just the cactus leaves evolved into thorns for several reasons. The most obvious is the defence mechanism. Thorns protect the cactus from being eaten by most animals. Another is sun protection: Some cacti have so many long, narrow thorns they look like hair. These help to protect the cactus from drying out. Thorns can also catch condensed water from the air to water the plant. Thorns are a quite practical thing indeed! Ouch!

133

The thorns of cacti are actually organs

THE FOOD OF T

CREATE

134

135

136

THE FUTURE IS NOW!

At the end of their exciting adventure, Sam and Lily are bravely entering the world of tomorrow. With more and more people living on this planet and more and more environmental issues, we need to change the way we eat. Experts and scientists are revealing a lot about the future of food to Lily and Sam: How better bacteria will be bred to grow more and better food, for example. It's all in the making as we speak!

RETRO TUNES WITH NEW FOOD? SOUNDS LIKE A HIT!

Salad grown on the International Space Station high above earth? Not that easy!

YOU CAN'T ORDER TAKEAWAY ON MARS? DARN!

VEGGIES FROM OUTER SPACE

If we want to live on other planets like Mars, we must make sure the space explorers get there healthy and in top shape. That's why astronauts on the International Space Station examine how zero gravity affects plants and veggies in outer space. It's not exactly an easy process: Plants need a very specific amount of gravity and sunlight to grow. Once we are able to build a civilisation on Mars, top priority will be producing foods such as fruits and vegetables. An apple a day keeps the Mars doctor away, too!

EVEN TODAY, RESEARCHERS ARE THINKING ABOUT THE FOOD WE WILL BE EATING IN THE FUTURE. SOME OF IT HAS ALREADY ARRIVED IN THE SUPERMARKETS – SPORTING MORE LEGS THAN YOU MIGHT THINK!

MEAT MADE FROM PLANTS

More and more people are deciding to eat less meat or no meat at all. Reducing the amount of red meat you eat can be good for your health, but a lot of people might find it difficult to give up. A pickle? Not for the food of tomorrow! More and more companies have emerged producing a kind of meat substitute which is made of plants – and pretty close to actual meat. It consists of many different ingredients like proteins from plants such as soy, pea and even rice. It's a good way to reduce meat consumption and help the environment.

Believe it or not: This is not meat!

137

I'M READY FOR A PLANT-BASED PARTY! YEAH!

Insects might play a huge role in our future diet!

FOOD WITH SIX LEGS

Dig this: Insects are thought to have been eaten in this world since the dawn of humanity. And while it's still strange or maybe even gross for some of us to think about eating beetles, ants or crickets, it's super common and popular in quite a lot of countries and among animals. It's good for the environment, too: Insects don't need much space to grow and generate far fewer greenhouse gases than conventional farming. What's more, they contain protein and are actually quite tasty when fried or baked!

Dig in: More than 2,000 species of insects are considered edible!

Did you know?

INSECT BURGERS ARE A THING!

WHEN IT COMES TO INSECTS, THE FUTURE OF FOOD IS ALREADY HERE: BURGERS WITH PATTIES MADE FROM OR WITH INSECTS ARE ALREADY HITTING THE SHELVES IN SUPERMARKETS IN GERMANY AND SWITZERLAND! NEXT TIME YOU AND YOUR FAMILY ARE BUYING GROCERIES, LOOK OUT! MAYBE INSECT BURGER PATTIES OR INSECT PASTA MADE IT INTO YOUR LOCAL SUPERMARKET AS WELL.

138

No fairy-tale: Burgers with insects are a thing now!

IF I CAN KISS A FROG, I CAN EAT A GRASSHOPPER. NO PROBS!

YOUR TRADING CARDS ARE COOL FOR SWAPPING WITH FRIENDS AND THAT'S NOT ALL! YOU CAN PLAY TWO FAB GAMES WITH THEM TOO.

PLAY WITH YOUR CARDS

For 2 to 5 players

GAME 1: LILY'S MAU-MAU

WHAT YOU NEED:

The best way to play the game is to collect as many cards as you can.

BASIC RULES

At the beginning of a game, five cards are dealt to each player. The rest of the cards are put in the middle as a deck. Flip over the top card of the deck and set it aside to begin the discard pile. The player to the dealer's left goes first and places one card from his hand on the discard pile. A card may only be put down if it matches the colour, the number or the symbol of the last card placed at the top of the discard pile. For the action cards there are special rules (see below). If you can't put any cards down, you have to draw a card from the deck. If you still can't put one down, it's the next player's turn. If you only have one card left in your hand at the end of your turn, you have to knock on the table twice. If you forget, you have to draw two cards. The player who puts down all their cards first wins!

CARD FUNCTIONS

The figures determine the value of the card

This number shows which slot the card fits in your collector's album.

The frames determine the colour of the card

FIREWORK GUY

What began as a costume for Halloween quickly turned into an obsession. Firework Guy has to hide on bonfire night, though, just in case someone tries lighting his bottom!

ACTION CARDS

Draw two cards
Next player in sequence draws two cards, unless they can play another +2 card. The amount of cards the following player must draw adds up. Example: You play a +2, next player plays another +2, next player in sequence must draw four cards.

Colour change
Player declares next colour to be matched. This card may be discarded on any colour or number.

Take card back
If this card is played the player's opponent must take back the last card placed on the discard pile to the hand. The take back card is placed under the deck afterwards and player may put down another matching card.

Skip a turn
Next player in sequence misses a turn.

Joker
This card may be discarded on any other card.

55

1. Lilly turned over two cards that didn't match.

symbols/values do not match & Frame colours do not match

4. Sam turns over another card and remembers where the card with the same symbol and colour was.

Remember? Here is the matching card for Sam!

For up to 4 players

GAME 2: SAM'S MEMO

YOU WILL NEED ...

...as many pairs of cards with matching colours and the same value or symbol as you can find.

HOW TO PLAY

In this game you and up to three other players have to prove your memory skills and find all matching cards. Take all your card pairs that share the same value or symbol and colour and shuffle them. Lay them out face down on a table in rows. The youngest player starts by turning over two cards. If he has found two matching cards with the same colour and the same value or symbol, he takes them and may turn over another two cards. If they do not match, every player has to remember what was on the cards and where they were. Cards that do not match are put face down again in the same place. Now it's the next player's turn. Go on like that until no more cards are left on the table. The player with the most matching card pairs wins!

IMPORTANT!
ALWAYS REMEMBER THE LOCATION OF THE CARDS YOU HAVE SEEN!

2. Lily and Sam memorize the cards and their location on the table.
3. Lily replaces the cards face down.

5. He turns it over and takes the matching pair.

symbols/values match & frame colours match

6. It's still his turn and he goes on turning over two more cards.
7. He goes on until he turns over two cards that do not match. He replaces them face down again.
8. Now it's Lily's turn again.

If you turn over two cards with the same symbols/values but with different colours you do not have a matching pair.

It's also not a matching pair if you have the same colour but different symbols!

SOLUTIONS

Check the solutions of the Brain Teasers you didn't find on the corresponding pages.

P. 23

2	4	3	1
1	3	4	2
3	1	2	4
4	2	1	3

3	4	2	1
1	2	4	3
4	3	1	2
2	1	3	4

4	1	2	3
3	2	4	1
1	4	3	2
2	3	1	4

P. 27

P. 36

P. 32

P. 39

P. 42-43 14 FRUITS

P. 44
THIS BRICK HAS TO END THE SECOND ROW:

P. 49

K	X	Z	A	M	E	R	I	C	A
Y	Z	S	A	L	T	Y	G	N	W
D	E	L	I	C	I	O	U	S	X
Q	F	P	Q	Y	M	D	C	B	R
S	R	O	Z	X	O	L	Z	M	B
L	W	P	Z	J	V	L	X	S	X
T	X	C	K	Z	I	J	Q	K	T
F	M	O	Y	Q	E	H	D	X	C
Y	K	R	J	P	S	X	X	T	X
X	H	N	W	V	X	W	Z	Z	T

CREDITS:

Cover illustration: Evgenij Rybnikov, other illustrations: Natascha Römer, Evgenij Rybnikov, Jon Hughes
Brain Teaser: kuroksta/Shutterstock
8-9:   8-9: Mario Hösel, Panthermedia - imago images (2); Valentina Rychkova/stock.adobe.com; Edgar G Biehle, Nadiia 80 – Shutterstock (2)
10-11: Cezary Wojtkowski, hepko Danil, mihalec, Nitr- stock.adobe.com (4)
12-13: Francesca/stock.adobe.com; AlisLuch, CHAINFOTO24, Dreamer1904, Evan Lorne, Ian 2010, KasperczakBohdan – Shutterstock (5)
14-15: Aliaksei Lasevich, Pavlo Burdyak, StudioDFlorez, Tatiana Shepeleva, Yeti Studio - stock.adobe.com (5); kuroksta/Shutterstock
16-17: Eric Isselée, gitusik, Serhiy Kobyakov, Studio Romantic, Андрей К - stock.adobe.com (5); Stefano Barzellotti/Shutterstock
18-19: Barbara, desdemona72, Patryk Kosmider - stock.adobe.com (3); Pixel-Shot, Denys Koltovskyi, robuart – Shutterstock (3)
20-21: valet, ixaHub, valery121283, Yeti Studio - stock.adobe.com (4); AODDYOSK99, nimon, Pikoso.kz– Shutterstock (3)
22-23: Africa Studio, Anatoliy Sadovskiy, Sevendeman, xamtiw - stock.adobe.comn (4); pr2is, TOM…foto - Shutterstock (2)
24-25: levranii, Maurizio Milanesio, surangaw - stock.adobe.com (3); azure1, Umomos, Jiri Hera – Shutterstock (3)
26-27: Benno Hoff, betka82, BillionPhotos.com, CeHa, Chris Leachman, Fox, Martin, Petrov Vadim, ruslanshug, yvdavid – stock.adobe.com (10); anat chant/Shutterstock
28-29: adimas, Gone For A Drive., totajla - stock.adobe.com (3); kwest, Michal Pesata, Peter Galleghan – Shutterstock (3)
30-31: bidaya, byrdyak, gerasimov174, procy_ab, vectorpouch, sonyakamoz - stock.adobe.com (6); Rossillicon Photography/Shutterstock
32-33: MrMarvlus Visuals, bruno ismael alves, bportolano, LIGHTFIELD STUDIOS- stock.adobe.com (4); The Len/Shutterstock
34-35: ermess, kuvona, mbridger68, RAJCREATIONZS, Volodymyr - stock.adobe.com (5); Elana Erasmus, majeczka– Shutterstock (2)
36-37: ArTo, bajinda, Richard Carey, dpreezg - stock.adobe.com (4); marekuliasz, sirtravelalot, wildestanimal – Shutterstock (3)
38-39: a7880ss, famveldman, zphoto11, Oleksandr Kotenko, September - stock.adobe.com (5); David Osborn, VectorShots – Shutterstock (2)
40-41: Byron Ortiz, atoss, Daniel Vincek, Elvira, Good Start, naypong, Oleg Zhevelev, Petra Heveroch - stock.adobe.com (8)
42-43: Grafvision, Ildi, iprachenko, Luis Echeverri Urrea, paulmz - stock.adobe.com (5); Chatchawal Kittirojana, Gerald H, Keeb thoj, Photo By Naynon, Yakov Oskanov – Shutterstock (5)
44-45: alexpermyakov, eyewave, jaime, kotelnyk, Pavel Svoboda, Tatyana A. - somepie - stock.adobe.com (6)
46-47: daphnusia, eric, freshidea, LuckySoul, Sergey Ryzhov - stock.adobe.com (5); Dominique de La Croix, osArt – Shutterstock (2)
48-49: fergregory, kaiskynet, Vankad, yanadjan, Yeti Studio, Željko Radojko, Zoriana - stock.adobe.com (7)
50-51: freshidea, juliedeshaies, lblinova, lunamarina, Roman Stetsyk, italy Korovin - stock.adobe.com (6); LuckyStep/Shutterstock
52-53: cosmicvue, exclusive-design, freshidea, koldunova_anna, steheap, Whyona - stock.adobe.com (5) ; Fabio Sacchi/Shutterstock
56-57: Fox, Francesca – stock.adobe.com (2), sirtravelalot/Shutterstock

LEGAL NOTICE: Created, designed and produced for Sainsbury's Supermarkets Ltd. by Blue Ocean Entertainment AG, Seidenstraße 19, 70174 Stuttgart, Germany (Contact: CTW3@blue-ocean-ag.de) under license from the LEGO Group.

MIX
Paper from
responsible sources
FSC® C074543

Card Gallery

HOW'S YOUR COLLECTION COMING ALONG?

TICK OFF THE TRADING CARDS YOU'VE ALREADY STORED IN THIS ALBUM. NOW START TRADING WITH YOUR FRIENDS TO COMPLETE THE COLLECTION!

BANG